Changing the Mind of Your World

A call for IT and import/export contractors in developing nations to speak out

Manoj Tulsyani

ISBN: 1503040089
ISBN 13: 9781503040083

"You must be the change you wish to see in the world."
- Mahatma Gandhi

One

"Speak only if it improves upon the silence."

- Gandhi

When I was born in Ramesh Nagar, a small town in the western section of New Delhi, India, there were only about five million people living in the capital. Today there are twenty-five million.

That's like every family of four in a city suddenly expanding to a family of twenty. That's phenomenal growth, and not all of it good.

When I was a child, in the seventies, I would ride through the streets of Delhi and stare with fascination at the chaos of traffic around me: bicycle rickshaws, bright green and yellow three wheeled motorbike-taxis, automobiles, men carrying all manner of packages, lumber and furniture on their heads and shoulders, automobiles continuously honking at each other to no avail, even the occasional cow or bull sauntering along through the street, smelling every little crumb and stain on the pavement.

Lining the streets were the vendors, each with their own little table or stand, selling pants, shirts, shoes, spices, and food. There was *lassi* to drink, *ram ladoo* to eat with *naan* bread, and a thousand other snacks, confections and teas.

And there were the beggars and the homeless. They seemed to be everywhere. Women, children, thin little old men lying on the street with wrinkled hands extended toward me. Sometimes, if I was out early in the morning, I would see the city workers pushing their carts through the alleys, picking up the bodies of those poor souls who had not survived the night.

All of life – and death – seemed to me to take place in the streets of Delhi, and even though my family had a comfortable, but small apartment, isolated from the overwhelming poverty around us, every time I went out, I could see the struggle for so many people in my country just to stay alive.

Today the percentage of poor in India may be less, but because the population of the whole country, not just Delhi, has grown so fast, from 539 million in 1970 to 1.2 billion today, the total number of poor is staggering. Estimates of those who earn less than basic subsistence range from 360 million – a conservative figure reached by the Indian government after they lowered the poverty criterion – to 600 million – by more realistic and objective sources that measure poverty by a higher and more accurate poverty line.

Most agree that the reduction in the percentage of poor in India has been the result of the rapid economic growth, especially since 1991 when the Indian government allowed new foreign investment in the country. As more jobs have been created by overseas firms in the country, Indian workers' wages from those jobs have allowed them to spend more within the local economy and thereby raise, albeit in minutely small increments, the overall standard of living in the country. A new, mostly high tech middle class is being born.

Even as a child, when I rode to the outskirts of the city, I would see the concrete high rises being built, one after the other, for families from this new middle class to move into in order to escape the impoverished chaos of the inner city. There were green lawns and little parks and even fountains and pools in these neighborhoods. It seemed to me a different world than the one ten kilometers to the east which I lived in, even though both were still Delhi.

Many agree that the authoritative bureaucracies created since the seventies by the Indian government to implement economic and social reforms within the country– including plans for the construction of these new high rise neighborhoods which continue to be built in Delhi today – may have actually pushed the economy into collapse and increased the country's poverty with their endless procedural confusion and departmental red tape. These bureaucracies are made up of India's old middle class, as rigid in their value systems and as punitive in their treatment of the poor as were the British, from whom they inherited many of their values. The unwavering practice by this old middle class of these harsh codes – originally under British rule, but today as well – has been necessary, they have felt, for them to hold on to their comfortable, but precarious status quo.

The end result of their governance is a Delhi today that in the heart of the city looks remarkably similar to the neighborhoods I grew up in forty years ago. Street traffic moves from chaos to grid-lock and back hourly, a menacing tangle of electric wires is suspended over life in the street and across the hodgepodge of corrugated iron and colored signs on the facades of the sometimes crumbling buildings, and the green and yellow motorbike taxis, bicycle rickshaws and human backs and shoulders are still the most prominent means of transportation through the streets.

Occasionally a cow is still seen sauntering along the pavement looking for scraps of food to lick up and chew or puddles of water to drink. In the early morning the bodies of those who did not survive the night are still carted away.

As overwhelming as the impoverished and squalid sights have been on the streets of Delhi, they often seemed safer to me than the tortured life I had within the walls of our own small apartment. My father worked as a judge for the Indian government, and that same authoritative and closed-minded attitude so prevalent in the Indian bureaucracies dictated his behavior toward his family as well. The suffering we children experienced seemed worse to me then, because it was mine, than the horrors of the many anonymous others I observed in the streets.

Like the country's old bureaucratic middle class, especially government workers, my parents gave priority to their own needs and welfare, but neglected the health and well being of those who entrusted their care to them. In our case, it was my brother and I, who they treated like servants or slaves or, sometimes, criminals.

The government may have given tiny daily handouts to the homeless beggars on the streets, but there was still never enough food to prevent many of them from having their corpses carried away the next morning. Although my brother and I woke up alive each day of our youth, we too often suffered from a lack of food, not to mention a lack of the love and care that would have nurtured us as we grew.

I was frequently kept locked in my room for days without any meals after some boyish behavior that did not meet my father's approval. At one point, after an extended period of deprivation, I ended up with blood in my stool and worms in my stomach, and I had become weak enough that I had difficulty standing. My uncle Bhagwan discovered me in this condition and took me to the hospital. He probably saved my life by doing so, but his caring for me put him on the wrong side of my father's punishing demeanor and Bhagwan was permanently exiled from the family for having interfered with my father's harsh punishment.

My elder brother, too, had constant arguments with our parents, especially my father, and he suffered as well from the stress of his constant run-ins with them. My brother was the most sympathetic of the family to my mistreatment and his protection of me led to much of the stress he experienced from our parents as they ridiculed him for being so supportive of me.

Horribly, he died in a motorcycle accident when I was still young, and I've always wondered if the constant emotional abuse he received from my father hadn't made him unstable and therefore much more prone to having that kind of accident.

Perhaps because of the unhappiness of my home life, I threw myself into my studies in high school and I did achieve success in all my schooling. In my twelfth grade physics exam I "topped" in the entire city of Delhi – meaning my grade was the highest of all in the city school system. I was momentarily elated, and I even began to feel like a little celebrity while I was being interviewed by the different newspaper agencies sent to my home to cover this major city news.

My fame and new confidence was short-lived, however, as my parents took most of the credit for my achievement as the reporters held their microphones and made notes with their pens and pads of everything my parents had to say about me from our living room's divan. I could only listen to them speak, silently, from the edge of the room.

My topping in Delhi physics did get me into engineering college, though, and soon I was learning all about computers in my classes and labs. I had already become fascinated by calculators and other small electronic gadgets, even telephones, as I was growing up, and as a youngster I could see how they could simplify life and make so many things easier for people.

Their potential to help humanity seemed to me in such stark contrast to the grim life I saw every time I went out into the streets of New Delhi, and I not only began to figure out just how they worked, which satisfied me immensely, but I began to envision what could be done with them to benefit the lives of others, as well.

I took an interest in scientific calculations and soon after I entered engineering college, I was learning the basics of Fortran and making program conversions form Pascal to C. After that I began creating word processing software for documentation and, because of my skills and my newfound interest in helping people, I began mentoring and tutoring other students in their studies.

Although I had been silent through most of my unhappy life at home, in college I could begin to speak out to my classmates. It felt good.

I ended up doing a lot of networking and building up a strong social circle around me and despite the continuing stress at home, I achieved some success in school and was often awarded with an invitation to work on advanced projects there.

By the time I graduated, I had gained a reputation that helped me get my first job. A company in Delhi which provided support for pharmaceutical packages hired me, and as happy as I was to have a good job and be making enough money that I could envision getting my own apartment, I soon began to see that I may have been being taken advantage of.

The owner had begun making more and more frequent trips to America, Germany and France to secure contracts, and although that brought in more cash flow and established a secure future for the firm, he worked those of us who were already there harder and harder to complete the ever increasing number of contracts. At first I started working evenings, then nights, and then I would often have to work around the clock to complete some of the most pressing deadlines.

I knew the company's profits were soaring with all the new work, but my pay remained the same. I went to the owner and asked for a raise. I spoke out for the first time, but my request was denied. I continued working these arduous hours until finally, exhausted and fed up with my slave-like existence, I threatened to quit. Only then was I given a raise.

I learned at that moment that not only does one need to speak out about unfairness in the work place, one sometimes needs to speak out about it loudly and often.

My IT skills continued to increase with the more sophisticated projects I was doing and my career finally hit a huge upswing when I was hired by Tata Consultancy Services. There too, however, I found that the company itself, like most of the large IT employment agencies, made a huge margin of profit, but continued to pay their staff for each project only a small portion of the income they received.

We were, of course, being paid far more than the impoverished masses in the streets of Delhi around us, and, as part of the new middle class, we were spreading the money from our paychecks out into the general economy of the country, but we were still being taken advantage of by the firm.

It was true, I discovered, that Tata had the expense of maintaining a large pool of candidates in order to be prepared for the ebb and flow of work, and that not all of these workers were doing projects or making money at the same time. However, I also saw that the company assigned the most projects to a small, highly skilled and reliable group of IT personnel, like myself, and the long hours and intense pressure that ensued from that cost saving by Tata meant that the most competent of us, ironically, ended up suffering the most in that environment.

The more I saw how the industry worked and how unfair some of its practices were – not just in the little companies like the one I had first worked at, but also at the large, international corporations that hired foreign labor – the more I wanted to be compensated fairly and to be put on an even playing field with other IT workers internationally. I began applying for jobs in the United States, but even though I was offered two jobs, I was not able to get a visa for either.

Once my application for a visa in the U.S. had been rejected twice, I was not eligible to apply again for two years.

I then started applying for jobs in Australia and Singapore, and I quickly got my first job offer with Singapore Computer Systems for the most expensive and most prestigious IT project in Singapore at that time. After that project, I worked for Cap Gemini and Reuters Asia and, with the exception of my very first job, I have since been working with large multinational companies throughout my career.

I did often speak out about the disparity I sometimes saw between a worker's value and his or her compensation, but now, with this book, I have decided to speak out more loudly yet.

The number of poor in India, be it three hundred million or six hundred million, demonstrates a violation of basic human rights that is unconscionable. The situation in other developing nations in Asia and Africa is similar.

As Earth's economy is transformed into a global market, care needs to be taken that workers in developing nations are not only compensated fairly, but are respected for the jobs they do, because it is this workforce that will share its income with the local economy and slowly bring entire countries up to a standard of living that recognizes the value and the importance of every human being.

Today the situation in India is intolerable. Besides the mammoth numbers of poor, the infrastructure of the entire country is still a failure. Public electricity is unavailable for large blocks of time, even in India's major cities. Urban sanitation is in many areas nonexistent and its absence breeds widespread disease.

Compulsory education, itself a human right per Article 26 the U.N.'s Universal Declaration of Human Rights, cannot be guaranteed in this kind of poverty and missing social infrastructure, even though it is universal education that will eventually help raise the populace out of its crippling poverty.

Other human rights from the Universal Declaration also continue to be ignored: equal pay for equal work (Article 23), some leisure time, not endless work hours (Article 24) and an acceptable standard of living, food, clothing and housing (Article 25), to name just a few.

Even more basically, per Article 22, everyone is entitled to a realization of the economic, social and cultural rights indispensable for his or her dignity. A walk today along two blocks of the streets of inner New Delhi shows how far India's poor are from even being able to imagine that right, let alone enjoy it.

The problem in India, and elsewhere, is monumental.

Speaking out, even speaking out loudly, sometimes feels like bailing out the ocean with a thimble. However, if one does nothing, one knows the problem will get worse, and one becomes guilty by complicity of inaction and of the consequent worsening of the problem.

By doing something, no matter how small a thimble one uses, there is hope.

Please speak out along with me through the tools I offer in this book, and speak out loudly.

Two

Speaking out about the problem, loudly or not, involves understanding exactly what the problem is.

Is it simply the greed of multinational corporations that take advantage of developing nation workers by paying them less and working them longer in substandard conditions so that corporate profits remain staggeringly healthy?

Certainly there have been instances of that brand of corporate abuse, such as the Silicon Valley high tech company, Electronics for Imaging, paying eight Indian workers $1.21 an hour while working them 122 hours per week without overtime pay. The company reported it "unintentionally overlooked" California law that dictated they should have been paid them the eight dollar an hour California minimum wage.

The company ended up paying more than $43,000 in back wages and penalties because someone spoke out loudly enough for the authorities to hear.

Electronics for Imaging had been paying these workers the same wages – and paying them in rupees, not dollars – that they would have received in their normal jobs in their home city, Bangalore, the new Silicon Valley of India. Ironically, though, what they were being paid while in California was still nearly four times more than what the minimum wage laws in India would have required them to be paid in Bangalore.

In other words, a high tech firm employing workers in India for the same tasks they did in America can get away with paying them even less than the paltry $1.22 an hour they were being paid – albeit illegally – in California.

The Universal Declaration of Human Rights, Article 23, demands equal pay for equal work. That rings true as a fair precept to be applied to all workers internationally, but there is a frequently unexamined variable in the application of this right, and that variable underlines the fact that the "problem" here is not necessarily simply one of corporate greed.

The designation of a legal minimum wage, country by country, is a step forward in our planet's history toward the global elimination of worker abuse, as has been the United Nations' Declaration of Human Rights, but given the disparity of minimum wages, country by country, one can see that the application of Human Right number 23 tends to be done only within the employment arena of each individual country.

Look at the above disparity, for instance, between the minimum wage in the original Silicon Valley in America, and in Bangalore, India.

The minimum wage in India tries to guarantee that each IT worker doing the same task within the country be paid the same wage, regardless if he or she is employed by a native Indian firm or a multi-national corporation. However, multinational corporations have been able to take advantage of this disparity in minimum wages from one country to another by employing developing nation workers at far lower wages than in the multinational company's home country.

Equal pay for equal work only applies locally, not globally.

Nonetheless, because of this very disparity, multinational companies' investments in developing nations and their workforce have been instrumental in raising the standard of living in those countries. Not only do local workers have more discretionary income to spend in the local economy by being offered new jobs by foreign investors – thereby benefitting other local businesses – but the investment of capital expenditure for facilities and infrastructure by the multinational firms themselves and the increased tax revenue of the host countries from them also help raise the country's standard of living.

As these multinational companies play a greater and greater role in dictating the world's economy, the playing fields expand from strictly local ones, internal to each country, to a global one. As that global economic arena continues to expand, more voices such as ours will speak out about how "equal pay for equal work" should be applied fairly on a global, not just a local level.

The more workers are educated about the disparities that exist, the more loudly they will learn to speak out, and the more carefully multinational companies will listen and begin to establish a true parity for all workers internationally

While multinational companies may not necessarily be seen as the golden goose to developing counties, the fact is that their continued overseas investments have helped bring up from abject poverty a substantial segment of the planet's population. As multinational companies – many of which have higher revenues than most developing nations – forge a stronger global economy, they also foster an increase in the standard of living in local economies.

Our purpose here is to acknowledge that, but also to speak out for the even larger percentage of humanity which still suffers from debilitating poverty and to help bring a new parity of equal wages for equal work on a global, not just a local playing field. We recognize we must speak out precisely about these disparities. We don't want to kill the goose that's laying the golden egg. Instead, we want to help that goose lay even more of these golden eggs of investment and employment which will continue to help raise the standard of living in developing nations around the globe.

We just want it to be done fairly.

But what is fair?

What is the right balance between enough corporate profit to promote expansion into cheaper labor markets and provide new employment and tax revenue within a developing nation without take unfair advantage of those less expensive laborers by underpaying and overworking them?

Here, too, the solution, like the problem, may not be a simple one.

The situation today with the H-1B guest worker visa in the United States provides an apt international focal point for the complicated and sometimes conflicting protests about wage and employment disparities within multinational firms. The H-1B visa was devised by the American government to allow American high tech firms to bring in from overseas highly educated and trained tech workers to fill job openings when, it was presumed, the American labor market could not provide those resources. A quota was set of 85,000 visas, 20,000 of which were for post-graduate degree holders.

Foreign workers who fill these high tech slots in American firms can legally be paid less through the temporary guest visa parameters than American workers doing the same work. As American firms do not need to prove that they have not been able to fill the high tech slots with native American workers, many well trained American workers, particularly in the IT field, have spoken out and accused firms like Microsoft of hiring foreign workers to cut costs, thereby undercutting American workers.

Highly trained foreign workers, on the other hand, have spoken out to protest the fact that they are being paid less than their American counterparts, even though they are doing the same software engineering work as native U. S. workers.

Complicating the issue even further is the fact that overseas temporary employment agencies have been securing visas for foreign workers who are not highly trained so that they can fill American workforce slots for less skilled, lower paying jobs. This, of course, opens the doors even further for new employment opportunities for developing nation workers, but at the same time even more American workers may be being bumped out of employment by these foreign workers.

My old employer, Tata Consultancy Services of Mumbai, is one of the leading IT employment agencies applying for and receiving H-1B visas for its Indian subscribers. Tata and other temporary employment agencies have inundated the U. S. with applications for H-1B visas, not just for the high tech positions the visa program was designed for, but for less skilled IT applicants who end up not being employed by the tech giants – Microsoft, Intel, Amazon and Google – that employ the bulk of the post-graduate visa holders. These less skilled foreign workers become employed instead at American outsourcing firms that perform more pedestrian software tasks.

Again, the irony here is that this gives even more Indian workers an opportunity to make a better income than they otherwise could in their native India and flow it back into the Indian economy as they send large portions of their American paychecks back home to their families, as most India workers do. At the same time they are being "taken advantage of" by these outsourcing firms like Tata that now have an extraordinarily cheap labor source and an extraordinarily high profit margin. Meanwhile, American workers are being kept unemployed by the obvious fiscal advantages to these non high tech firms for hiring inexpensive foreign workers.

As one American software consultant – who himself, even more ironically, is a naturalized citizen who now has been unable to find work because of overseas H-1B visa competition – complained, he used to be upper middle class, but now he has become lower middle class because of the low cost, untrained Indian workers being brought in. Of course, these low cost Indian workers themselves are now moving up with their families from the Indian lower class to the new middle class because of the higher wages, by basic Indian standards, from their H-1B employment.

It should be noted that the major multinational high tech employers like the four named above, Microsoft, Intel, Amazon and Google, do have a far greater percentage of highly trained post-graduate degreed H-1B workers than do the outsourcing firms. These firms tend to use the temporary visa program to expand their ability to create the technical innovation that provides the cornerstone for the continuing expansion of the global economy and the global benefits of a raised standard of living internationally because of that expansion.

It is the story of our planet.

The first textile mills in the 18th century took advantage of new technological innovation, as well, to develop the machine tools and manufacturing processes that began the Industrial Revolution. These industries started the first major expansion of both local and global economies on the planet through the technical innovation in those early factories, crude as it may now seem to the sophisticated innovation of, say, today's semiconductor industry.

Today, just as earlier on the planet, technology has continued to expand both local and global economies as well as the living standards of a multitude of ordinary people who have benefited by the growth of these multinational companies.

And just as there were workers who were taken advantage of by employers in textile mills and other early industrial enterprises, so too have there been injustices within the modern high tech arena.

Voices spoke out about these earlier injustices, too. Trade unions were formed to protect workers from being underpaid and overworked, conditions improved, an international workforce expanded, and eventually international minimum wage sanctions were drawn up and international human rights declarations were made, even if there is still a long way to go toward ensuring these humane safeguards are applied broadly.

The Industrial Revolution began in England and England, too, was the home of the first multinational company, the British East India Company, which brought to India the beginnings of a new economy and along with it, a pejorative labeling as "wogs" the population of that "developing" nation. This condescending attitude can still be seen today in India and elsewhere in the "old" middle class and its treatment of the "new" middle class. To some extent this cultural attitude underlies the justification of mistreatment of Indian workers and others today and the misuse of them by those members of the "old" middle class who populate the government and large, bureaucratic corporations like the multinational employment firms such as Tata Consultancy Services.

In the history of the planet itself since the Industrial Revolution – and in developing countries, as well, more recently – there is a successive formation of one new middle class, which then achieves a new status quo and, through fear or misplaced authority, digs in to entrenched and rigid values to become an impediment to further social change, even though it was change itself that raised them to their new standard of living and new power and status within society.

Then, historically, new agents of change make their voices heard and rally to take their place as the "new" middle class, but they too risk becoming a new "authority" as well and often find themselves equally entrenched in the protection of their new status quo. They suddenly find, if their eyes are open and they are alert, that they've become an "old" middle class themselves.

The rotation continues throughout history, but the standard of living of the people around them, globally or locally, continues to rise through the application of technical innovation.

Today we need to speak out as members of the "new" middle class of employees of multinational firms, both in the IT and import/export other industries, just as our predecessors on the planet have, so that we can continue to bring parity in wages, treatment and standards of living for all workers in our fields within the global, not just the local playing field.

We are the new agents of change and, if we keep our eyes open and stay alert, we will remain agents of change by continuing to speak out about global disparities and by not falling into the comfortable trap of becoming a new status quo.

In short, you and I need to remember to keep changing the minds of our world, globally and locally.

Three

So, how do you speak out?

Who do you speak out to?

Will it have any effect?

Any one of you who loves your community and wants to raise its standard of living can improve your neighborhood, your city, your country by speaking out, even though at first you might feel you are bailing the ocean with a thimble.

There is the ancient tale about the inventor of chess who went to the emperor of India to introduce him to his new game. The emperor was so delighted with the clever game that he said he would grant the inventor any wish. The inventor, a bright man, said his wish would be to have the emperor place one grain of rice on the first square of the chess board, two grains on the second, four on the third, and then keep doubling the number of grains of rice on each of the remaining sixty-four squares.

The emperor granted his wish – until the state treasurer informed the emperor that the total number of grains of rice would be more than eighteen quintillion, more rice than India had ever produced throughout its already long history of rice growing.

At that point, the emperor had the inventor of the chess board beheaded.

There will be no beheadings here for speaking out, but the tale illustrates the power of exponential growth.

If I tell you about the disparity of wages for IT workers in the world, let's say, and you tell one person, and then each of us and each of them tell another person and so on, the entire population of the planet would be informed just after we passed the half way point of squares on that chessboard – if we were using the sequence of sixty-four squares to tally the results of this public relations campaign.

Beyond that personal approach, you can, of course, also speak out to government officials, corporate management, media people, and anyone in a position of public influence who might forward your message.

In other words, you can, in actuality, have a great effect on the world, no matter the size of your thimble, just by speaking out…even if you just start by speaking out to your close associates or through your own social media use.

The question then becomes, what do you say?

Here are six points that will begin to help alleviate the disparity in pay and treatment of workers from developing nations and that will also help raise the standard of living of developing nations.

So, speak out. Speak out loudly. Speak out often.

- Education

The first thing you can do is further the education of your co-workers in the IT field or import/export industries about the international disparity in wages and the benefits for them individually, for their city and for their country, by speaking out also and thereby helping to change that disparity.

You can do this informally – over coffee or a drink or at family meals – or more formally – through letters, e-mail, blogs or social media.

What's most important is simply getting the word out, making the situation known. Although you may immediately only have an effect on a small number of people, the exponential effect of their educating others and those others educating others will be powerful.

We can speak very loudly indeed if all of our individual voices eventually come together in one large united voice of "we."

- Raising the minimum wage standards within the IT industry and for other import/export workers

If we focus on international parity of wages for workers in the IT industry and for other import/export workers from developing nations, we can bypass the somewhat meaningless minimum wage standards that have been set, country to country.

One criterion we can start with is the minimum pay standard the United States legislature has set for foreign workers employed in America through the H-1B visa. Per U.S. law, those workers must be paid at least seventeen percent of what their American counterparts are paid for doing the same job.

Although that's far higher than the minimum wage set by law in India itself, it is an almost criminally small percentage of what these H-1b workers deserve to be paid.

If that percentage was raised, just to start with, from seventeen to even forty or fifty percent, there would still be enough cost saving incentive for high tech American firms to hire well trained foreign workers from developing nations. Even more importantly, the additional income these workers earned would, at the very minimum, triple the amount of money they sent home for their families to spend in their local economies back in India.

If those workers maintained the living expenses they now had in America without increasing the percentage they paid from their wages, they would be able to send home five to ten times the amount they now do. That influx of money spent in the local Indian economy would itself help to exponentially raise the standard of living there, as it would in any other developing nation

• Profit sharing by multinational firms for workers in developing nations

It is no secret that multinational firms are profitable. In 2012, ninety-two Fortune 500 companies increased their offshore holdings by over 500 million dollars each to take advantage of the profit available overseas, primarily through a cheaper labor force. The top ten overseas investors – including Microsoft, Apple, Google, IBM, GE, Merck – increased their offshore profits collectively by $107 billion.

That's the increase, not the profit itself. Microsoft, for instance, earned $86.7 billion worldwide in 2014 and had a net profit of $22 billion. That figure would still leave considerable room for profit sharing by its overseas employers to compensate them for their lower minimum wages.

Besides a cheaper labor market, foreign taxes are also an incentive for multinational investment in overseas markets. Although American firms must pay the same corporate tax rate for earned overseas income as for their domestic income, the foreign taxes paid are subtracted from their payments to the U.S. government. Because other countries may be less exacting in their taxes, the amount of foreign corporate taxes a multinational pays may be proportionately less overseas, and that is a great incentive for them to invest in developing nations. American multinational firms can take advantage of local tax loopholes for saving money, and that provides them with a great incentive for overseas investment even beyond the cheaper labor they can employ.

For those non-American multinational companies, too, the lower foreign tax rates in some foreign countries make foreign investment in them even more attractive.

For instance, Ireland had a corporate tax rate for foreign investors of 10.58 percent in 2010. Ireland attracted $21 billion of foreign investment that year and it received $2.3 billion in taxes paid on that income. India's corporate tax rate in that year, on the other hand, was 32 percent, one of the highest on the planet. It received only $2.8 billion in foreign investment and reaped only $920 million in taxes.

Given the fact that India is reported to have the largest highly trained tech workforce in the world – 1.7 million – shouldn't India lower its tax rate in order to attract more foreign investment and gain more tax revenue just as lower tax rate countries like Ireland have done?

In 2006 the tech service sector in India contributed to 40 percent of the country's GDP, yet the tech services workforce was only 25 percent of the country's labor pool. In other words, 25 percent of the workers in India were producing 40 percent of the country's revenue.

By lowering the foreign investor tax rate and perhaps even requiring a profit sharing proportionate to foreign investment, India should be able to attract far more foreign investments than they do now and, even with a profit sharing variable, still offer significant overall profit to multinational corporations. The country would also be protecting and rewarding its IT tech services workforce appropriate to their contribution to the country's production.

Even if the government did not mandate profit sharing by multinationals investing in India, the reduced tax rate would still make profit sharing a greater possibility – and would compensate workers for lower paying jobs – by those American multinational firms operating in India.

- IT professionals be given the right to purchase legal software and licenses

$2.9 billion worth of unlicensed software was installed in India in 2013, according to the nonprofit organization BSA. India was second only to China in the dollar amount of unlicensed software sold in Asia in 2013. Today it is estimated that almost $800 billion in exported IT products are in jeopardy due to the pirated software, and that will require consumers to spend as much as $150 billion in security measures to protect the illegal software from malicious programs.

Only thirty-three percent of companies in India have any written policy that requires the use of properly licensed software.

The BSA report suggests that if the amount of pirated software could be reduced by a mere ten percent, there would be an increase in revenue of $700 million to the IT industry and $900 million for other related industries. As the reliability of legitimate software increases, even by just that ten percent, and additional 15,000 jobs would be added in the IT industry in local software, services and channel companies.

The government would also receive more tax revenue from the legal software, which will help build the nation, and Indian software development companies would enjoy higher revenue through the increased sale of legal software.

You not only should speak out loudly to companies to begin to introduce policy that penalizes any use of pirated software, but you can also warn any workforce personnel you know personally who are jeopardizing revenue and reputation by currently using unlicensed software. They may believe it is cheaper in the short run to employ the pirated material, but you can show them how in the long run they are actually cutting their own throats.

- Trained professionals need to make themselves known as the valuable components of the workforce which they are as prime contributors to the raising of their country's standard of living

Ever since Lord Macauley wrote in the 1830's that he never found anyone who "could deny that a single shelf of a good European library was worth the whole native literature of India and Arabia" and ever since the world's first multinational, the East India Company, started instructing Indians in the "superior" language, English, the inhabitants of developing nations have taken a bad rap.

British colonialists even manufactured false stories of the rape of their women in order to help justify their continued intervention in India, and we "third world" inhabitants became the "White Man's Burden," as Rudyard Kipling so deprecatingly put it, in a phrase that also has been widely used to justify imperialism as an honorable enterprise.

The then "new" Indian middle class, raised to a higher social status by their real and imagined authority as Indian government workers, began to use that justification for their own punitive treatment of their countrymen. That attitude, which is now the "old" middle class one, can still be observed in Indian government workers and corporate officers today as they continue to try to protect their own authority and hold on desperately to their status quo.

A poll published by the reputable American newspaper *The Washington Post* in 2013 found, ironically, that India is the second most racist country in the world after Jordan. Forty-three percent of Indians polled said they would not want to live next to a neighbor of a different race.

In our current fight to raise our own respect-ability and positive stature as a crucial component of the India workforce, we may have met the enemy and, as they say, "the enemy is us."

In order that we achieve the respect and admiration that we IT and import export workers deserve, we need to police our own ranks by speaking out against any pejorative and self-invalidating comments we hear, especially when it comes from within our own group.

We need to speak out, often and loudly, by championing our value to the country as the "new" middle class dedicated to changing those fixed ideas we still find around us which are hampering the accelerated improvement of the standard of living of India. We need to promote the fact that although we are only 25 percent of the workforce, we produce 40 percent of India's GDP.

The Universal Declaration of Human Rights recognizes that if people are to be treated with dignity, they require economic rights, social rights and the rights to cultural and political participation, along with civil liberty. Human Rights Article 2 states that everyone is entitled to those rights "without distinction of any kind, such as race, color, sex, language, religion, political or other opinion, national or social origin, property, birth or other status."

We need to speak out on any channel against "old" middle class discrimination as well as speak out in favor of "new" middle class value.

- Links to put on your social media pages

The biggest help you can provide is promoting the information in this book to your friends via your emails – while copying me on the cc list – and on your social links on facebook, twitter, youtube, linkedin and any other websites.

My own email contact is:
tmanoj100@noveltyservices.org

Also, please list the following links in your own social media:

http://www.amazon.co.uk/dp/1503040089
http://www.amazon.de/dp/1503040089
http://www.amazon.es/dp/1503040089
http://www.amazon.fr/dp/1503040089
http://www.amazon.it/dp/1503040089

Please also use the following form to gather other volunteers, and when you have collected their information, you can forward it to me at my e-mail address, tmanoj100@noveltysystems.org.

I would also like to acknowledge the following early volunteers and promoters who have already started to change the mind of our world:

Rajesh, Veena, Monika, Rajiv, Tulsyani's, Lalwani's, Gehanis, Suri's, Punjabi's, Dinesh Bhatia, Vipul Bhardwaj, Arun Varshney, Ajay Wadhawan, Sandeep Dhingra, Rajesh Jain, Pankaj Jain, Pankaj Aggarwal, Harpreet Mouron, Suresh Thakur,

Vishal Bhardwaj, Kailash Advani, Soni Nihal, Nikesh Modi, Chakravarthy Dova, Jitender Kwatra, Rajiv Gehani, Nilesh Patel, Manish Takyar, Jayesh Patel, Saurabh Agarwal, Asha Shah, Nilesh Sahita, Anurag Jain, Ajithan Vidyadharan, Ranga Rao, Pankaj Luthra, Gagan Oberoi, Ajay Gupta, Sushil Lamba, Pradeep Gupta, Balwant Jain, Sachin, Ajit Singh, Ravi Vig and Kapil Aggarwal

I Want to Volunteer

	Volunteer Name	Phone (Home)	Phone (Cell)	Email	Area of Expertise/ Interest	Days/ Times Available
1						
2						
3						
4						
5						
6						
7						
8						
9						
10						
11						
12						
13						
14						
15						

Four

"First they ignore you, then they laugh at you, then they fight you, then you win."

- Gandhi

I would like to help you win. When you win, we all win.

After my childhood of isolation and uncertainty, I was happy to find that the IT skills I had achieved by the time I was in my second year of college gave me a new confidence in life, a confidence both in myself and in being able to help other people. The interest I could then comfortably take in other students – in real, live people, not just in the "safe" electronic objects of my youth – without any longer feeling the fear of rejection, allowed me to find a new satisfaction in life from my efforts to mentor and tutor others.

The networking I did then and the strong circle that I then became part of has given me friends and associates who have remained with me throughout my life.

Whatever help I can now give you in your career, I would like to give.

Certainly my experience in the IT field makes my help more valuable to other IT workers, especially those just starting their careers and uncertain of exactly what paths to take, but I also offer myself to any developing nation worker who wishes to change the mind of our world.

I've provided a sample resume here, based on my own experience, and you may be surprised how detailed it is. There is an idea floated around that a resume should only be one page long, maybe just over a page at the most.

Perhaps in other fields that is true, but in my experience, when applying for an IT job, the technical staff who will ultimately be responsible for hiring you need to know exactly what skills and experience you have.

What does need to be short is the cover letter for your resume.

The cover letter is what should be less than a page. It goes to a Human Resource person or a recruiter who usually has a limited technical background and wants only to know your experience and talents generally before your resume is passed on to the technical supervisor who will carefully go over all the specific details of your technical and educational experience.

You can use my sample resume as a template for your own.

Please feel free to contact me at tmanoj100@ noveltysystems.org for any question you have about your career which you think I might be able to help you with.

In other words, speak out to me.

Sample Resume

Experience Summary

- Install, configure and tune Cloudera Hadoop as big data hub for the Global Wealth Management at Merrill Lynch as a part of client wellness initiative. Use Hadoop client, hive, sqoop, flume and Java mapreduce programs for data ingestion from various data sources, such as flat files, DB2, Oracle, MSSQL, MySQL into hdfs, hive and hbase. Write MapReduce generic patterns for input/output format, filter, sort, joins, HiveQL queries, Pig scripts to do analytics on the data loaded. Interface Tableau for client to do analytics. Install, Configure Hortonworks HDP, Implement security authentication using Kerberos, wire security for Ambari
- Design and develop Big Data Real Time application using Apache Kafka, Hadoop

Storm, Streaming with java/python on Hortonworks HDP.

- Install and configure Hadoop on Amazon EC2
- Design and development of data warehouse using appliances such as Netezza, Greenplum and traditional platforms such as Oracle, DB2, MSSQL, MySQL in all phases of SDLC, MDM tools, ETL tools using AbInitio, Informatica and custom perl shell scripts and java programs.
- Migration of data warehouse from traditional platforms such as Oracle, DB2 to Greenplum and Netezza, writing BRD, DFD, Functional Specifications, ETL specifications and provide 24X7 support of Oracle, Sybase and MSSQL server databases.
- Working knowledge with DB appliance, such as Netezza, Greenplum architectures, Pivotal HD Hawq, data distribution, tuning, NZ/plsql and pgplsql
- Working experience on the Configuration and Map Reduce programming, Architect, Setup, Install and Administration of custom Hadoop (HDFS, Mapreduce, Hive, Hbase, Pig, Sqoop, Hawq) – Individual Components, Pivotal HD, Cloudera and Hortonworks implementations.
- Writing backend database applications and reporting using J2EE, Spring and Hibernate framework, JSPs and servlets, MVC model.

- Composite Software Data Virtualization experience at the NYSE as a Solutions Architect and developer, working experience in equities, capital markets, derivatives, compliance and regulatory requirements.
- Client profile includes Merrill Lynch, Prudential, NYSE Euronext, Citigroup, AXA Financial Inc, Cap Gemini Asia Pt. Ltd. (Citibank Projects), Reuters Asia Pt. Ltd., Singapore Computer Systems, and Tata Consultancy services. Working experience in equities, capital markets, derivatives, fixed income, global wealth management, risk markets, insurance, re-insurance, compliance.
- Extensive experience in design/ development of Data Warehouse, PL/SQL, shell scripting, various relational databases and database appliances, ETL tools, BI tools
- Highly motivated team player possessing outstanding interpersonal skills, strong project planning experience with a willingness to take on challenging assignments.

Project Experience
<u>DataFrom – DateTo –Merrill Lynch (Pennington, NJ) Hadoop / Big Data - Lead Consultant</u>
- Install, configure and tune Cloudera Hadoop as big data hub for the Global Wealth Management at Merrill Lynch.
- Install, manage and administration of Cloudera big data hub platform. Implement

Namenode high availability, security authentication using Kerberos, configure multi-tenancy between batch and real time processing

- Smoke test various components - Smoke Test various services with test cases – HDFS, MapReduce, Pig, Hive, Hbase, Sqoop, Flume, Oozie, Storm, Management Services.
- Design the data ingestion framework depicting the use of various Hadoop eco-system tools, RDBMS, decision tree and workflow.
- Configure Cloudera environment. Develop and use Java MapReduce programs, generic patterns for filters, sort, join, Sqoop, Flume and JDBC drivers to do data ingestion from various RDBMS.
- Use Hadoop client, hive, sqoop, flume and java mapreduce programs for data ingestion from various data sources, such as flat files, DB2, Oracle, MSSQL into hdfs, hive and hbase with few custom transformations. Develop Java mapreduce programs, pig scripts for filtering, transformation, sorting and joins to do customer analytics across various data sets and dimensions. Develop and build mapreduce programs using IDE and command line, use maven for build and packaging.
- Write pig scripts, macros, udfs to analyze various data sources using filters, grouped

and ordered data sets, develop re-usable macros using Pig Latin itself to analyze top customers across various dimensions.

- Write HiveQL to do analytical queries, load data in the Hadoop data hub.

DateFrom – DateTo – Prudential (Woodbridge, NJ) Big Data Architect - Lead Consultant

- Migrate Data Store from SQL Server to Greenplum DW, data migration, ETL, perl/shell scripting
- Work on Oracle Data Warehouse, ETL, PL/ SQL, perl/shell scripting
- Define and Configure Metadata
- Deploy Pivotal/ HAWQ (Hadoop Distribution). Migrate data to HAWQ for analytics. Write Java MapReduce programs to load data and perform analytics using generic filters, sort, aggregates, develop mapreduce patterns. Use maven build and packaging tool and eclipse IDE. Deploy jar files.
- Write HiveQL, Pig scripts to do analytics across retirement portfolio. Write Pig Latin macros, pig udfs using java mapreduce. Integrate java mapreduce classes with pig scripts. Develop pig scripts as prototype for generating analytics. Convert pig scripts to java mapreduce programs. Write generic mapreduce filter using java generics, generic parser using regex pattern.

- Write pgplsql ETL programs, shell scripts, Data Validation/Comparison scripts
- Configure and implement daily and monthly cycle.
- Enhance DB2 database applications. Write stored procedures and triggers.

DateFrom – DateTo - NYSE Euronext (Wall Street, NY), Data Warehouse Director

- Design and develop Ab Initio graphs, Informatica Workflows/mappings, custom perl, shell, SQL, Oracle PL/SQL, Greenplum PL/pgSQL, Netezza PL/SQL scripts to transform and load data into Data warehouse running on Oracle RAC, Netezza and Greenplum. Develop, NZ PL/SQL, Greenplum Postgres SQL, PL/pgSQL scripts to generate data for analytics and Reporting using Business Objects Universe and OBIEE presentation, Logical/Physical modeling, MDM hub.
- Write Surveillances and custom ETL (data format, coding changes, e.g. ebcdic to ascii, text manipulation, Filters, Joins, Rollups, Normalization) using C and Java programming using cloud infrastructure custom developed with thread worker pools, database connection pools, use concurrent java programming, Generics.

- Perl, Java, Unix awk and shell scripting to perform simple text, data transformations, regex expressions.
- Write C++ UDFs for analytics, thread, connection and memory pools.
- Web development using J2EE, Spring, Struts2, Hibernate frameworks, JSP/Servlet MVC model, Web Services (JAX-WS and JAX-RS) to maintain operational data, cloud infrastructure, hosts, databases, operational statistics, post analytical data.
- Design, build and maintain Greenplum Architecture deployment and documentation with redundancy, failover, master mirroring, segment mirroring, data distribution, GP database parameters tuning
- Backing up and restoring database. Parallel Loading and unloading data using gpload and gpfdist. Creating and managing database, database objects, users, roles, privileges, udfs, pgplsql procedures, Performance monitoring and query optimization
- Work with Composite as a data virtualization and federation tool to connect various heterogeneous data sources (Oracle, Netezza and Greenplum) deploying all our JDBC drivers for data sources at composite server and presenting clients (ETL Tools and reporting Tools) as single data source using composite ODBC driver.

- Use both composite SQL functions, joins, optimizations and also database functions, joins, optimization depending upon the efficiency of the composite SQL and database SQL and the requirement to access heterogeneous data sources to get the results. Use standalone Java Programs with Composite JDBC Driver to get the required data in the standalone applications. Composite stack helped put all the data source drivers and complexity of accessing data sources at one place and presenting clients with one single ODBC or JDBC driver to access composite.

- Write Functional Specifications, Data Flow Diagram, database design using relational and dimensional data modeling, working with multi dimensions, design star schemas using Erwin, compare different model versions, reverse engineering, translate logical design into physical structures. Design and develop ETL Workflows using ETL tools.

- Design, install and manage OLTP Oracle and PeopleSoft Application database systems, Oracle Real Application Cluster (RAC) 10g and upgrade to 11gR1 running on 6 node cluster with VLDB (50 TB) optimizing with different LUN sizes and interconnect bonding, extensive database and application tuning, experience using sql trace, ADDM, SQL outlines, SQL Profiling, wait events and I/O tuning, design and implement backup and recovery procedures for production and business continuity/DR sites using RMAN hot backup, write shell scripts for automation of daily activities, implement hot standby using SRDF, Data Guard and replication technologies.

- Load data warehouse with Ab Initio Graphs, Informatica Workflows and open source ETL Tools to connect to heterogeneous DB environments, data cleansing, writing mappings using sort, rank, lookup, joiner, filter, aggregate, sequence generator transformations.

- Manage/mentor Data Warehouse team of onsite and offsite developers and DBAs.

- Tune SQL scripts, PL/SQL packages using sql trace, automatic workload repository, wait events, sql profiling, stats generation and improve query performance from 4 hours to less than 10 minutes.

- Perl scripting for text transformations, regex, search/replace. In C, write programs with dynamic bonding, passing functions as parameters, using pointers, dynamic memory allocation and management, writing daemons to service requests, writing programs for Unix shareable libraries.

- Develop upgrade strategy, design data migration strategy from legacy data warehouse using a combination of transportable tablespaces, export/import and copy over database link. Implement ASM to get the maximum throughput by striping the data files across LUN.

- Manage critical production issues on a daily basis; provide 24X7 support of development and production RAC environment.
- Design and implement backup Solution for the database using physical BCV/split backup, RMAN hot backup and logical backup using export/import.
- Write shell scripts for automating data loading using hand shake feature, database and RAC alerts, monitoring of space, creation of tablespaces, partitions, profiling, stats generation.

DateFrom – DateTo - Citigroup (Warren, NJ), Citigroup Architecture and Technology Engineering AVP

- Global cost optimization using consolidation and virtualization techniques. Presenting proposals for new technologies with ROI, forecasting and analyzing cost reductions and budgeting, presentations, consulting and global deployment of technology solutions.
- Gather cloud infrastructure, database related requirements for application deployments from various business sectors. Evaluate vendor products meeting the collected requirements.

- Project management and technical experience in evaluation and selection of computing, clustering, network, storage, disaster recovery, replication, backup and archiving technologies, drafting and enforcing standards across all business sectors globally
- Recommend software stack based on the matrix of business requirements, financial and technical factors, write job profiles/ roles, business justifications, conduct interviews, project planning, identify/mitigate risks, and deliver project on time within budget.
- Perform gap analysis between the cloud and database infrastructure requirements vs. vendor products and develop in-house custom solutions. Implement infrastructure, capacity planning, business sector charge-back, configuring and allocating virtual resources to business sectors, applications.

DateFrom – DateTo - AXA Financial Inc (NY, NY), Oracle/SQL Server/PeopleSoft/Sr Database Analyst

- Install, configure and maintain Oracle8i and Oracle9i RAC Databases, MS SQL server
- Write custom ETL using C and Java programming using cloud infrastructure custom developed with thread worker pools, database connection pools

- Perl, Java, Unix awk and shell scripting to perform simple text, data transformations, regex expressions.
- Java core development, Web Development using J2EE, JSP/Servlet MVC model, Web Services to query post analytics and etl data.
- Write C++ programs for custom ETLs connecting to heterogeneous data sources.
- Write shell scripts to automate daily tasks for monitoring, backup and alerts.
- Design data warehouse using relational and dimensional data modeling, working with multi dimensions - location, product, organization, time, design star schema using Erwin, compare different version models, translate logical design into physical model, generate DDLs.
- Build data warehouse with Informatica to connect to heterogeneous DB environments, data cleansing, writing mappings using sorting, rank, lookup, joiner, filtering, aggregation, sequence generator transformation. Use ODBC, oracle transparent gateways, IBM data Joiner, flat files and Informatica for data exchange across multiple databases.
- Write PL/SQL procedures, functions, triggers and SQL Analytic Functions. Write exception handlers, autonomous transactions, dynamic SQL and dynamic PL/SQL. Write UNIX shell scripting for batch

processing, automation of daily activities and ETL processes. Work with Informatica to connect to heterogeneous DB environments, data cleansing, writing mappings using sorting, rank, lookup, joiner, filtering, aggregation, sequence generator transformations, mid-tier application administration, install, configure and tuning, portal, single sign-on, forms and reports services, application deployment (jar files), apache web server, implement security by disabling http, using only https, implement VeriSign certificate, password protect html pages.

- Create, configure and tune SQL databases, implement snapshot and transactional replication, configuring and managing linked servers using SQL Server Enterprise Manager/management studio. Use SQL profiler, SQL Analyzer to tune user queries.
- Configuring and working with database tools such as Toad, SQLStation and OEM.

DateFrom – DateTo - Cap Gemini (Singapore), Credit Risk Management System (CRMS) PM / DBA

- Design system to facilitate the Credit Facility Maintenance, Credit Approvals, security & collateral document maintenance, sub-allocation of credit lines, booking online earmarking transaction, generation of availment, offering, deferral tickets and Risk Exposure Reporting.

- Design and implement Credit Risk Management System (CRMS). Collect requirements from different countries. Rollout CRMS to 12 Asia Pacific Countries with various constraints, country specific requirements and customization. Involved in all aspects of project life cycle from collecting requirements to implementing & supporting the application, development on Oracle D/B using Oracle Forms, SQL*PLUS, PL/SQL, PRO*C, D/B triggers, stored procedures, packages, user exits. Database Administration activities and maintenance of 26 instances, performance tuning.

Education

DateFrom - DateTo	Master Of Technology (Software Engineering) National University of Singapore
DateFrom - DateTo	Bachelor Of Engineering (Electronics & Communications) Delhi College Of Engineering, India

Technical Experience

Business Sectors	Working experience in equities, capital markets, derivatives, fixed income, global wealth management, risk markets, insurance, re-insurance, compliance and regulatory requirements.

Big Data / Distributed Computing	Custom Hadoop eco-system (Hdfs, Mapreduce, Hive, Hbase, Pig, Sqoop), Pivotal HD & Cloudera– 2 years+ at Merrill Lynch, Prudential and NYSE Grid Computing – 5 years+ at NYSE
Data warehouse Appliance	Netezza, - 5 Years at NYSE Greenplum – 6 Years at NYSE and Prudential
Data Virtualization	Composite – 5 Years at NYSE
RDBMS	ORACLE – 15+ years at Merrill Lynch, NYSE, Citigroup, AXA DB2 – 5 years+ at Prudential, NYSE, Citigroup, AXA Sybase ASE – 3 years at Citigroup MSSQL Server – 6 years+ at NYSE, Citigroup, AXA MYSQL – 5 years+ at NYSE, Citigroup, AXA
Database Design & ETL	Erwin, Ab Initio, Informatica – 6 yeaars+ at NYSE and AXA Custom ETL using C, C++, Java programming, Perl, Unix Shell, awk and java scripts
Business Intelligence	Business Objects, OBIEE – 6 years+ at NYSE, Citigroup and AXA
Database tools	Aqua Data Studio, Quest Toad / Central, Foglight, BMC Patrol, SQL Station, pgadmin, OEM Grid Control, Oracle SQL Developer, Oracle Forms – 15 years+ at Merrill Lynch, Prudential, NYSE, Citigroup, AXA

Web Technologies	Web Services, JSP, Servlets, XML, Web Services JavaScript - 5 years+ at NYSE and AXA
Web Frame Works	Struts, Spring, Hibernate - 5 years+ at NYSE and AXA
Middle Tier / Application Servers	Composite, IBM WebSphere, BEA Weblogic, Jboss, Tomcat, GlassFish
IDE/ Development tools	Eclipse, NetBeans, maven, ant, pvcs, svn, git – 6 years+ at Merrill Lynch, Prudential, NYSE, Citigroup, AXA
Operating Systems	Linux, Unix, Solaris, Red Hat, Windows, Ubuntu, Open/VMS
Development / Database / Programming	C, C++, Java, Perl, SQL, NZplsql, Oracle PL/SQL, Greenplum plpgsql, shell scripts, java script, html, xml – 10 years+ at Merrill Lynch, Prudential, NYSE, Citigroup, AXA
Client/Server	PeopleSoft 8, Developer2000, PowerBuilder, SQLWindows - 5+ years at AXA
Case / Data Model Tools	Erwin4.1, UML, ObjectOry, Silverrun
Software Development	SDLC, Object Oriented analysis and design, Use Case design, Prototyping – 15+ years at Prudential, NYSE, Citigroup, AXA

References

1. References
2. References
3. References
4. References
5. References